By the

CW01432025

Prayers for Noahides: Community Services and Personal Worship

Edited by:

Dr. Michael Schulman and
Chaim M. M. Reisner

Directors, Ask Noah International

Emmanuel A. Villegas

*President, QCUHO Noahide Community,
the Philippines*

Including selected prayers authored by

Rabbi Moshe Weiner
and
Rabbi J. Immanuel Schochet

2

Approved by
Rabbi Moshe Weiner, Jerusalem
Overseeing Rabbinical Authority

ISBN 978-1-7323735-2-5
Copyright © 20'19-20'20 by Ask Noah International
Aug. 21, 20'19 / 20 Menachem Av, 5779

For information contact:

Ask Noah International
Email: SevenLaws@asknoah.org
Internet: www.asknoah.org

*This volume contains translated verses of
Hebrew Scripture and should be treated accordingly.*

Cover design courtesy of Brandyn Ashing.

Other publications from Ask Noah International:

The Divine Code, Fourth Edition

Seven Gates of Righteous Knowledge (English and Russian)

*Prayers, Blessings, Principles of Faith, and
Divine Service for Noahides,* 7th Edition
(Dutch, English, Spanish, French, Portuguese, Indonesian)

*To Perfect the World: The Lubavitcher Rebbe's Call
to Teach the Noahide Code to All Mankind*

CONTENTS

DAILY PRAYERS AND BLESSINGS

PRAYERS FOR SPECIFIC NEEDS AND REQUESTS

PSALMS AND PRAYERS FOR ELUL, TISHREI, ROSH HASHANAH AND HANUKAH

INTRODUCTION

The intent for this book is to provide personal, family, and communal prayers that are appropriate for Gentiles who follow the Torah's Seven Commandments for the Children of Noah. Care has been taken that the prayers included here do not encroach on the spiritual heritage of the Jewish people, and there is no attempt being made to establish additional obligations for Gentiles beyond what is required within the Noahide Code.

We hope that this publication will be a useful guide, and the expanded selection of Psalms and verses from the Hebrew Bible is offered as a resource for heartfelt prayers and praises to God. Our hope is that this will bring each worshiper to a closer, more personal relationship with the Holy One, blessed be He.

The QCUHO Noahide community in the Philippines (Qehilat Chasidie Umot Ha-Olam) which inspired this resource has done well by establishing places and times for communal prayers for their numerous local branches. We sincerely thank Mr. Emmanuel Villegas, a leader of their organization, who originally had looked to the traditional Jewish liturgy (the Orthodox *Siddur*) to find guidance for orderly and uniform prayers in the growing number of QCUHO Noahide synagogues. By submitting his draft version to Ask Noah International for review, editing and rabbinical authorization, he brought to our attention the practical need for daily or weekly prayer services for Noahide communities.

The QCUHO prayer booklet was subsequently revised, authorized and published in the Philippines. We have used that version to a large extent in this present work,[1] while continuing to expand on the daily prayers for Noahides that had been recommended by Rabbi Moshe Weiner, the overseeing Rabbi of Ask Noah International, and Rabbi J. Immanuel Schochet, o.b.m. We also offer the e-book and pocket-size printed booklet titled *Prayers, Blessings, Principles of Faith, and Divine Service for Noahides* (7th Edition). The following guidelines for prayer are a summary of details provided there and in the book *The Divine Code* (Third Edition) by Rabbi Moshe Weiner.

---

[1] Works consulted for translation of Biblical verses: *Siddur Tehillat HaShem* (English & Hebrew), pub. Merkos L'inyonei Chinuch; *The Complete Artscroll Siddur (Ashkenaz)*, pub. Mesorah Publications; *The Stone Edition Tanach*, pub. Mesorah Publications; *Tehillim Ohel Yosef Yitzchak with English*, pub. Merkos L'inyonei Chinuch; *Tehillim* (The Artscroll Tanach Series), pub. Mesorah Publications.

GUIDELINES FOR PRAYER

The universal obligation to pray is to ask for one's physical needs, but the true main purpose is to connect with the Creator. A constant connection with God is also an essential human need – that God should be with a person in all his ways, and that all of his ways should be fitting for this connection. The prayer itself is a connection, made through conversation, requests, and praises to God, Who hears the prayer of all and also provides this spiritual need. With this in mind, a main part of prayer is concentration on the greatness of God and the Truth of His Existence, to set these ideas in one's heart in all areas of life.

Gentiles have no set liturgy of prayers that they are obligated to follow. Rather, each individual can pray to the One God in his own words, in a language that he understands. It is proper to include recitation of appropriate excerpts from the Book of Psalms by King David, of blessed memory, since the Psalms are all prayers to God that were composed with holy inspiration and which incorporate all the essential needs and righteous spiritual emotions that people have.

One should express his prayers to God in speech and not only in thought, so he will earn the merit of doing a good deed in the service of God. A Gentile may pray at any time of day, in any fitting words he chooses. But he should not pray to God if he is in a house of idol worship, and he should be careful not to use prayers that idolaters composed for their liturgies. With this caveat, any prayers may be sung with appropriate melodies.

One's prayers should be said honorably, so it is meritorious to pray in honorable clothing and with clean hands. One should not pray in filthy clothing, or unclothed, or in the presence of others who are unclothed. One should also not pray where there is a bad smell, or in a lavatory or bathing room, or within about 6 ft (1.8 m) of foul material. In those situations, if there is a great need to pray but one cannot move to a place that is acceptable for prayer, it is better to pray in one's heart and not say God's name in any language in such a place.

THE IMPORTANCE OF CHARITY BOXES

The use of small containers for depositing coins for proper charity is a righteous practice that is greatly encouraged for Gentiles as well as Jews. The Divine service of charitable giving dates back to Abraham, as God said (Genesis 18:19): "For I love him [Abraham] because he commands his children and household after him that they shall keep the way of God to do charity and justice…"

Charity is an act of goodness and kindness, and Gentiles also have an obligation to give charity and to be concerned about helping those who are physically in need. This also applies to helping those who are spiritually in need, by financially supporting outreach to more people about observance and study of the Noahide Code. The merit of giving charity helps protect one from harm and prolongs life, especially by giving any amount before praying – when a person can benefit from this extra merit which helps his prayers to be well received and answered by God. And now more than ever, "Great is charity, because it brings the Redemption closer."

A Summary of the 7 Noahide Commandments

1. BELIEF IN GOD: **Do Not Worship Idols.** The Creator of the physical and spiritual worlds is unlimited and unified in His Oneness, and everything comes from Him. He cares about and judges our deeds, and His Providence is all-encompassing. The worship of anything other than God perverts the purpose for which we are created.

2. RESPECT GOD AND PRAISE HIM: **Do Not Blaspheme His Name.** To curse in this way is the ultimate disloyalty to God, Whose holy Name we must revere. Let your soul feel its awe of Him.

3. RESPECT HUMAN LIFE: **Do Not Murder.** Manslaughter is an attack on the image of God – the human soul – that He invested in every living human being, whether born or unborn, healthy or ill.

4. RESPECT THE FAMILY: **Do Not Commit Forbidden Sexual Acts.** Accept God's eternal boundaries on human desire. The Torah teaches that incest, adultery, homosexuality and bestiality are forbidden, and that this should be extended to all sexual practices that are destructive to individuals or the society at large.

5. RESPECT THE PROPERTY OF OTHER PEOPLE: **Do not steal.** Respect the rights of others. Income and property are granted by God, so we must seek to acquire these honestly, and not by theft.

6. RESPECT ALL CREATURES: **Do not eat flesh that was severed from an animal before it died.** Although transgression of this command applies specifically for land mammals and birds, it is also meant to teach the importance of not inflicting unnecessary pain or suffering on any creatures.

7. CREATION OF A JUDICIAL SYSTEM: **Pursue Justice.** Establish and uphold righteous courts of law. A consistently fair and effective system of criminal and civil laws creates a peaceful society that can receive God's blessings.

DAILY PRAYERS AND BLESSINGS

UPON AWAKENING IN THE MORNING

Upon awakening, a person should consider in Whose Presence he lies, being mindful of the Supreme King of kings, the Holy One, blessed be He, as it is said (Isaiah 6:3), "The whole world is filled with His glory."

After the proper personal preparations, one should begin the day by giving thanks to the Creator:

I offer thanks to You, living and eternal King, for You have mercifully restored my soul within me; Your faithfulness is great.

MORNING SERVICE
(WITH ADDITIONS FOR SATURDAY)

*It is proper to prepare for each prayer service
by washing one's hands.*

The prayer leader begins:

May my prayer to You, Lord, be at a time of favor;
O God, in Your abundant kindness, answer me with
Your true deliverance.[2]

Behold, the fear of the Lord is wisdom, and turning
away from bad is understanding.[3]

May the Seven Noahide Commandments of the
Torah be my guide, and may God Almighty be my
help.

---

[2] Psalms 69:14.
[3] Job 28:28.

All recite the prayer
"Adon Olom" (Lord of the Universe)[4]

Lord of the universe, Who reigned
before anything was created –

at the time when He made all by His will,
then was His Name proclaimed King.

And after all things will be uplifted,
the Awesome One will reign alone.

He was, He is, and He shall be in glory.
He is One, and there is no other
to compare to Him, to call His equal.

Without beginning, without end –
power and dominion belong to Him.

He is my God and my ever-living Redeemer,
the strength of my lot in time of distress.

He is my banner and my refuge,
my portion on the day I call.

Into His hand I entrust my spirit
when I sleep and when I wake.

And with my soul, my body too,
the Lord is with me, I shall not fear.

---

[4] A prayer from the traditional *Siddur* prayer-book liturgy.

***All stand and recite these words of blessing:**[5]*

Blessed is He Who spoke, and the universe came into being; blessed is He.

Blessed is He Who says and does.

Blessed is He Who decrees and fulfills.

Blessed is He Who creates all that exists.

Blessed is He Who has compassion on the earth.

Blessed is He Who has compassion on the created beings.

Blessed is He Who provides good reward to those who fear Him.

Blessed is He Who lives forever and exists eternally.

Blessed is He Who redeems and saves; blessed is His Name.

Leader: Give thanks to the Lord, proclaim His Name; make His deeds known among the nations. Search for the Lord and His might; always seek His Presence. He is the Lord our God; His judgments are over all the earth. Tell of His glory among the nations, and His wonders among all the peoples. The Heavens will rejoice, the earth will exult, and among the nations they will say: The Lord reigns![6]

---

[5] From the traditional *Siddur* prayer-book liturgy.

[6] I Chronicles 16:8,11,14,24,31.

All recite the following verses:

Give thanks to the Lord for He is good, for His kindness is everlasting.[7] Exalt the Lord our God and bow down at His holy mountain, for the Lord our God is holy. May You, Lord, not withhold Your mercies from me; may Your kindness and truth continually guard me. Lord, remember Your mercies and Your kindnesses, for they have existed for all time. Deliverance is the Lord's; may Your blessing be upon Your people forever.[8]

Leader: The Lord of hosts is with us; the God of Jacob is our eternal stronghold. Lord of hosts, happy is the man who trusts in You. Lord, help us; may the King answer us on the day we call![8]

All recite: Our soul yearns for the Lord; He is our help and our shield. For our heart shall rejoice in Him, for we have put our trust in His holy Name. May Your kindness, Lord, be upon us, as we have placed our hope in You.[9] Lord, show us Your kindness, and grant us Your deliverance.[10] Arise, be our help, and redeem us for the sake of Your lovingkindness.[11]

---

[7] I Chronicles 16:34.
[8] Verses of Psalms from the *Siddur* prayer-book liturgy.
[9] Psalms 33:20-22.
[10] Ibid. 85:8.
[11] Ibid. 44:27.

Leader: I have placed my trust in Your kindness, my heart shall rejoice in Your deliverance; I will sing to the Lord for He has dealt kindly with me.[12]

All recite Psalm 67:

For the choirmaster with instrumental music, a Psalm, a song. May God be gracious to us and bless us; may He make His countenance shine upon us forever, so that Your way will be known on earth, Your salvation among all nations. The nations will extol You, O God; all the nations will extol You. The nations will rejoice and sing for joy, for You will judge the peoples justly and guide the nations upon the earth forever. The peoples will extol You, O God; all the peoples will extol You, for the earth will have yielded its produce, and God, our God, will bless us. God will bless us; and all, from the farthest corners of the earth, will fear Him.

---

[12] Ibid. 13:6.

Psalms 92 and 93 may be recited on Saturday:

Psalm 92:

A Psalm, a song for the seventh day. It is good to thank the Lord, and to sing praise to Your Name, O Most High. To proclaim Your kindness in the morning, and Your faithfulness in the nights, with a ten-stringed instrument and with a lyre, with singing accompanied by a harp. For You, Lord, have made me happy with Your deeds; I sing for joy at the works of Your hand. How great are Your works, O Lord! Your thoughts are exceedingly profound. A boor cannot know, and a fool cannot understand this: when the wicked thrive like grass, and all evildoers flourish, it is in order that they may be destroyed forever. But You, Lord, are exalted forever. Indeed, Your enemies, O Lord, indeed Your enemies will perish; all evildoers will be scattered. But You will increase my might like that of a wild ox; I will be anointed with fresh oil. My eyes have seen my watchful enemies; when evildoers rise up against me, my ears have heard. The righteous will flourish like a date palm; he will grow tall like a cedar in Lebanon. Planted in the House of the Lord, they will flourish in the courtyards of our God. They will still be fruitful in old age; they will be vigorous and fresh – to declare that the Lord is just; He is my strength, in Whom there is no injustice.

Psalm 93:

The Lord reigns; He is clothed with grandeur; the Lord has clothed and girded Himself with might; He also established the world firmly that it shall not falter. Your throne is established from of old; You are eternal. The rivers have raised, O Lord, the rivers have raised their voice; the rivers have raised their raging waves. More than the sound of many waters, mightier than the waves of the sea, the Lord is mighty on high. Your testimonies are most trustworthy; Your House will be resplendent in holiness, O Lord, forever.

On all days, recite Psalm 100:

A Psalm for the thanks offering. Let all the earth sing in jubilation to the Lord. Serve the Lord with joy; come before Him with exultation. Know that the Lord is God; He has made us and we are His, His people and the sheep of His pasture. Enter His gates with gratitude, His courtyards with praise; give thanks to Him, bless His Name. For the Lord is good, His kindness is everlasting, and His faithfulness is for all generations.

Then recite the following verses:[13]

May the glory of the Lord be forever; may the Lord find delight in His works. May the Name of the Lord be blessed from now and to all eternity. From the rising of the sun to its setting, the Name of the Lord is praised. The Lord is high above all nations; His glory transcends the Heavens. Lord, Your Name is forever. Your remembrance, Lord, is throughout all generations. The Lord has established His throne in the Heavens, and His kingship has dominion over all. The Heavens will rejoice, the earth will exult, and among the nations they will say: The Lord reigns! The Lord is King, the Lord was King; the Lord shall be King for ever and ever.

---

[13] Selected from the traditional *Siddur* prayer-book liturgy.

The Lord has annulled the council of nations; He has foiled the schemes of peoples. Many are the thoughts in the heart of man, but it is the counsel of the Lord that endures. The counsel of the Lord stands forever, the thoughts of His heart throughout all generations. For He spoke and it came to be; He commanded, and it endured. Indeed, the Lord has chosen Zion; He desired it for His dwelling place. Indeed, the Lord will not abandon His people, nor will He forsake His heritage. And He, being compassionate, pardons iniquity, and does not destroy; time and again He turns away His anger, and does not arouse all His wrath.

Leader: Deliver us, Lord; may the King answer us on the day we call![14] Happy are those who dwell in Your House; they will yet praise You forever.[15] Happy is the people whose lot is thus; happy is the people whose God is the Lord![16]

---

[14] Ibid. 20:10.
[15] Ibid. 84:5.
[16] Ibid. 144:15.

All recite the following Psalms:

Psalm 145:

A Psalm of praise by David: I will exalt You, my God the King, and bless Your Name forever. Every day I will bless You, and extol Your Name forever. The Lord is great and exceedingly exalted; there is no limit to His greatness. One generation to another will praise Your works and tell of Your mighty acts. I will speak of the splendor of Your glorious majesty and of Your wondrous deeds. They will proclaim the might of Your awesome acts, and I will recount Your greatness. They will express the remembrance of Your abounding goodness, and sing of Your righteousness. The Lord is gracious and compassionate, slow to anger and of great kindness. The Lord is good to all, and His mercies extend over all His works. Lord, all Your works will give thanks to You, and Your pious ones will bless You. They will declare the glory of Your kingdom, and tell of Your strength, to make known to mankind His mighty acts, and the glorious majesty of His kingdom. Your kingship is a kingship over all worlds, and Your dominion is throughout all generations. The Lord supports all who fall, and straightens all who are bent. The eyes of all look expectantly to You, and You give them their food at the proper time. You open Your hand and satisfy the desire of every living thing. The

Lord is righteous in all His ways, and benevolent in all His deeds. The Lord is close to all who call upon Him, to all who call upon Him in truth. He fulfills the desire of those who fear Him, hears their cry and delivers them. The Lord watches over all who love Him, and will destroy all the wicked. My mouth will utter the praise of the Lord, and let all flesh bless His holy Name forever.

Psalm 146:

Praise the Lord! Praise the Lord, O my soul. I will praise the Lord while I live; I will chant praises to my God while I exist. Do not place your trust in nobles, nor in a human being, for he does not have the ability to bring deliverance. When his spirit departs, he returns to his earth; on that day, his plans come to naught. Fortunate is he whose help is the God of Jacob, he whose hope rests upon the Lord his God – Maker of Heaven and earth, the sea, and all that is in them, Who safeguards truth forever. He renders justice to the oppressed; He gives food to the hungry; the Lord releases those who are bound. The Lord opens the eyes of the blind; the Lord straightens those who are bowed; the Lord loves the righteous. The Lord watches over the strangers; He gives strength to the orphan and widow; He thwarts the way of the wicked. The Lord shall reign forever, your God, O Zion, throughout all generations. Praise the Lord!

Psalm 150:

Praise the Lord! Praise God in His holiness; praise Him in the firmament of His strength. Praise Him for His mighty acts; praise Him according to His abundant greatness. Praise Him with the sounding of the ram's horn; praise Him with harp and lyre. Praise Him with timbrel and dance; praise Him with stringed instruments and flute. Praise Him with resounding cymbals. Let the entire soul praise the Lord. Praise the Lord!

Blessed is the Lord forever, Amen and Amen.[17] Blessed is the Lord from Zion, Who dwells in Jerusalem; praise the Lord![18] Blessed is the Lord God, the God of Israel, Who alone performs wonders. Blessed is His glorious Name forever, and may the whole earth be filled with His glory, Amen and Amen.[19]

Leader:[20] Blessed, praised, glorified, exalted and upraised is the Name of the King Who rules over kings, the Holy One, Blessed is He, for He is the First and the Last, and aside from Him there is no

---

[17] Ibid. 89:53.

[18] Ibid. 135:21.

[19] Ibid. 72:18-19.

[20] Cf. traditional Ashkenazi *Siddur* prayer-book liturgy.

[other] God.[21] His Name is exalted beyond every blessing and praise.[22] Blessed is the Name of His glorious kingdom for all eternity. Blessed be the Name of the Lord, from this time and forever.[23]

All stand while the leader chants:

Bless the Lord Who is blessed.

All respond: Blessed be the Lord Who is blessed for all eternity.

Our Father, merciful Father, Who is compassionate, have mercy on us, and grant our heart understanding to comprehend and to discern, to perceive, to learn and to teach, to observe, to practice, and to fulfill Your will with love. Enlighten our eyes in Your wisdom, cause our hearts to cleave to Your Seven Commandments, and unite our hearts to love and fear Your Name; and may we never be put to shame, disgrace or stumbling. Because we trust in Your holy, great and awesome Name, may we rejoice and exult in Your salvation. Lord our God, may Your mercy and Your abounding kindness never forsake us.[24]

---

[21] Cf. Isaiah 44:6.
[22] Cf. Nehemiah 9:5.
[23] Psalms 113:2.
[24] Adapted by Rabbi Moshe Weiner from the traditional *Siddur* prayer-book liturgy.

Meditation: As Noahides, when we accept and follow the ways of God based on Torah with the faithful of Israel as our guides, we link our destiny to theirs. It is appropriate to confirm this solidarity by verbally accepting God's Unity and Kingship:

Accepting God's Unity and Kingship:[25]

Almighty God, we accept upon ourselves that which is written in Your Torah:[26] "You shall know this day and take to your heart that the Lord [alone] is God, in the heavens above and on the earth below – there is none other!"

We affirm the precepts of: "You shall love the Lord, your God, with all your heart, and all your soul, and all your might;" and "Fear the Lord, your God, and serve Him, and in His Name [alone] shall you vow;" and, as it says, "Fear God and keep His commandments, for that is a person's entire duty."

---

[25] This and the following "Amidah" prayer were composed by Rabbi J. Immanuel Schochet.
[26] Deuteronomy 4:39.

"Amidah" (Standing) Prayer

All recite quietly and devoutly, without interruptions:

Blessed are You, God, the Supreme Being Who bestows abundant kindness.

Please endow us graciously with wisdom, understanding, and knowledge.

Please accept our repentance, and forgive us for our errors and sins.

Grant complete healing for all our wounds and ailments.

Bestow upon us all the needs for our sustenance from Your bounty.

Hasten the day of which it is said: "God will be King over the entire earth; in that day God will be One and His Name One;"[27] "For then I will turn the peoples to pure language, so that all will call upon the Name of God to serve Him with one purpose;"[28] and "They will not harm or destroy on all My holy mountain, for the earth will be filled with knowledge of God as water covering the sea bed."[29]

Hear our voice, God, our merciful Father, have compassion upon us and accept our prayers in mercy and favor. *(Other requests may be inserted here.)* Blessed are You, God, Who hears prayer.

---

[27] Zechariah 14:9.

[28] Zephaniah 3:9.

[29] Isaiah 11:9.

All assembled say the following
"Prayer of the Repentant"
(optional for an individual who prays alone)

O God, I have erred, sinned and willfully transgressed before You, and I have done that which is evil in Your eyes, especially with the sin(s) of … *(quietly state the specific sins or errors).*

I am sincerely ashamed of my sins, and I repent and firmly undertake not to do so again.

Please God, in Your infinite grace and compassion, forgive my sins and transgressions and grant me atonement, as it is written: "Let the wicked abandon his way and the man of iniquity his thoughts; and let him return unto God, and He will show him compassion, and to our God, for He will pardon abundantly."[30] And it is written: "Do I desire at all that the wicked should die, says the Lord, God; it is rather that he return from his ways and live!"[31]

---

[30] Isaiah 55:7.
[31] Ezekiel 18:23.

Group Torah Study (optional)[32]

Recite before the study begins:

For from Zion shall go forth the Torah, and the word of the Lord from Jerusalem. Blessed is He Who in His holiness gave the Torah to His people Israel. Blessed is the Name of the Master of the Universe! I do not put my trust in man, nor do I place my reliance on an angel, but only in the God of Heaven Who is the true God, Whose Torah is truth, Whose prophets are true, and Who performs numerous deeds of goodness and truth. I put my trust in Him, and I utter praises to His holy and glorious Name.[33]

Group Torah-Study Session (*sitting*)

Recite when the group study is concluded:

The Torah which Moses placed before the Children of Israel is a tree of life for those who hold fast to it, and those who support it are fortunate.[32] Its ways are pleasant ways, and all its paths are peace.[34] Who

---

[32] The halachic guidelines for Torah study by Noahides are published in *The Divine Code*, Part I, ch. 5, by Rabbi Moshe Weiner.

[33] Cf. traditional *Siddur* prayer-book liturgy.

[34] Proverbs 3:17.

is the man who desires life, who loves long life wherein to see goodness? Guard your tongue from evil, and your lips from speaking deceitfully. Turn from evil and do good, seek peace and pursue it.[35]

Psalms 19:8-15 may be recited here after the group study on Saturday:

The Torah of the Lord is perfect, restoring the soul; the testimony of the Lord is trustworthy, making the simpleton wise. The precepts of the Lord are just, rejoicing the heart; the commandment of the Lord is clear, enlightening the eyes. The fear of the Lord is pure, abiding forever; the judgments of the Lord are true, they are all righteous together. They are more desirable than gold, than much fine gold, sweeter than honey or drippings of honeycomb. Indeed, Your servant is careful with them; in observing them there is abundant reward. Yet who can discern accidental wrongs? Cleanse me of hidden sins. Also hold back Your servant from willful sins; let them not prevail over me; then I will be unblemished and keep myself clean of gross transgression. May the sayings of my mouth and the meditations of my heart be acceptable before You, Lord, my Rock and my Redeemer.

---

[35] Psalms 34:13-15.

On all days, recite Psalm 20:

For the choirmaster, a Psalm by David. May the Lord answer you on the day of distress; may the Name of the God of Jacob fortify you. May He send your help from the Sanctuary, and support you from Zion. May He remember all your offerings, and always accept favorably your sacrifices. May He grant you your heart's desire, and fulfill your every plan. We will rejoice in your deliverance, and raise our banners in the Name of our God; may the Lord fulfill all your wishes. Now I know that the Lord has delivered His anointed one, answering him from His holy Heavens with the mighty saving power of His right hand. Some [rely] upon chariots and some upon horses, but we invoke the Name of the Lord our God. They bend and fall, but we rise and are invigorated. Lord, deliver us; may the King answer us on the day we call.

All recite the following prayer [36]

(Bow while saying "We bend the knee".)

We bend the knee, bow down, and offer praise, before the supreme King of kings, the Holy One blessed be He, Who stretches forth the Heavens and establishes the earth, the seat of whose glory is in the Heavens above, and the abode of Whose majesty is in the loftiest heights. He is our God; there is none else. Truly, He is our King; there is nothing besides Him, as it is written in His Torah: "Know this day and take unto your heart that the Lord is God; in the Heavens above and upon the earth below there is nothing else." [37]

And therefore we hope to You, Lord our God, that we may speedily behold the splendor of your might, to banish idolatry from the earth – and false gods will be utterly destroyed; to perfect the world under the sovereignty of the Almighty. All mankind shall invoke Your Name, to turn to You all the wicked of the earth. Then all the inhabitants of the world will recognize and know that every knee should bend to You, every tongue should swear by Your Name. Before You, Lord our God, they will bow and prostrate themselves, and give honor to the glory of Your Name; and they will all take upon

---

[36] Cf. traditional *Siddur* prayer-book liturgy.

[37] Deuteronomy 4:39.

themselves the yoke of Your kingdom. May You soon reign over them forever and ever, for kingship is Yours, and to all eternity You will reign in glory, as it is written in Your Torah: "The Lord will reign forever and ever." [38] And it is said: "The Lord shall be King over the entire earth; on that day the Lord shall be One and His Name One." [39]

All recite: Indeed, the righteous will extol Your Name; the upright will dwell in Your Presence. [40]

---

[38] Exodus 15:18.
[39] Zechariah 14:9.
[40] Psalms 140:14.

PSALMS FOR THE DAYS OF THE WEEK

Levites sang these in the Holy Temple in Jerusalem. The first six were chosen for their relation to God's creative works on those days during the Seven Days of Creation.

Sunday: Psalm 24

By David, a Psalm. The earth and all therein is the Lord's; the world and those who dwell there. For He has founded it upon the seas, and established it upon the rivers. Who may ascend the mountain of the Lord, and who may stand in His holy place? He who has clean hands and a pure heart, who has not used My Name in vain and has not sworn deceitfully. He shall receive a blessing from the Lord, and kindness from God, his Deliverer. This is the generation of those who seek Him, who seek Your Presence – Jacob, forever. Lift up your heads, O gates, and be lifted up, everlasting doors, so the glorious King may enter. Who is the glorious King? The Lord, strong and mighty; the Lord, mighty in battle. Lift up your heads, O gates; lift them up, everlasting doors, so the glorious King may enter. Who is the glorious King? The Lord of hosts, He is the glorious King forever!

Monday: Psalm 48

A song, a Psalm of the sons of *Korach*. The Lord is great and exceedingly praised in the city of God, the mountain of His Sanctuary. Beautiful in landscape, the joy of the entire earth – Mount Zion, by the northern slopes, the city of the great King. In her citadels, God is known as a stronghold. For behold, the kings assembled; they advanced together. They saw and were astounded; they were terror-stricken, they hastened to flee. Trembling seized them there, pangs like a woman in difficult labor. With an east wind You shattered the ships of Tarshish. As we have heard, so have we seen in the city of the Lord of hosts, in the city of our God; God shall establish it forever and ever. God, we have been hoping for Your kindness within Your Sanctuary. Like Your Name, O God, so is Your praise to the ends of the earth; Your right hand is full of righteousness. Mount Zion shall rejoice; the towns of Judah shall exult, because of Your judgments. Walk around Zion and encircle her, count her towers. Consider well her walls, behold her lofty citadels, in order that you may recount it to a later generation. For this is God, our God, forever and ever; He shall lead us eternally.

Tuesday: Psalm 82

A Psalm by Asaph. God stands in the council of judges; among the judges He renders judgment. How long will you judge wickedly, always favoring the evildoers? Render justice to the needy and the orphan; deal righteously with the poor and the destitute. Rescue the needy and the pauper; save them from the hands of the wicked. They do not know and they do not understand; they go about in darkness; all the foundations of the earth tremble. I said, "You are angelic, all of you are supernal beings." But you will die as mortals, and you will fall like any prince. Arise, O God, judge the earth, for You possess all the nations.

Wednesday: Psalm 94

The Lord is a God of retribution; O God of retribution, reveal Yourself! Exalt Yourself, O Judge of the earth; render to the arrogant their recompense. How long will the wicked, O Lord, how long will the wicked rejoice? They continuously speak insolently; all the evildoers act arrogantly. They crush Your people, Lord, and oppress Your heritage. They slay the widow and the stranger, and they murder the orphans. They say, "God does not see, nor will the God of Jacob perceive." Understand, you senseless of the people; you fools, when will you become wise? Will He Who implants the ear not hear? Will He Who forms the eye not see? Will He Who chastises nations not punish? – He Who imparts knowledge to mankind. The Lord knows the thoughts of a person, that they are vanity. Fortunate is the man whom You chastise, O Lord, and from Your Torah You teach him – to grant him peace from days of trouble, while a pit is dug for the wicked. For the Lord will not abandon His people, nor will He forsake His heritage. For judgment will bring return to righteousness, and all those with upright heart will pursue it. Who will rise up for me against the wicked ones? Who will stand up for me against the evildoers? If the Lord had not been my help, my soul would have soon dwelt in the silence [of the grave]. If I thought that my foot was slipping, Your kindness, Lord, supported me. When my worrisome thoughts multiply within me, Your comfort delights my soul. Can a throne of evil be associated with You? Those who make evil into law? They join together against the soul of the righteous, and condemn innocent blood. But the Lord was my fortress, my God, the strength of my refuge. He will turn their violence upon them, and destroy them through their own wickedness; the Lord our God will cut them off.

Thursday: Psalm 81

For the choirmaster, on the *gittit*, by Asaph. Sing joyously to God Who is our strength; call out to the God of Jacob. Raise your voice in song, sound the drum, the pleasant harp with the lyre. Blow the ram's horn on the New Moon [of Rosh Hashanah], the day appointed for [Israel's] Holy Day. For it is a statute for Israel, the [day of] judging for the God of Jacob. He ordained it as a precept for Joseph when he went forth over the land of Egypt, when I heard a language that I did not know. [God says:] "I removed his shoulder from the burden; his hands were removed from the kettle. In distress you called, and I delivered you; you called in secret, and I answered you with thunderous wonders; I tested you at the waters of Merivah. *Selah.* Listen, My people, and I will attest to you; Israel, if you will listen to Me – no strange god shall be among you, neither shall you prostrate yourself to a foreign god. I am the Lord, your God, Who brought you up from the land of Egypt; open your mouth wide [with your requests], and I shall grant them." But My people did not heed My voice; Israel did not want [to listen to] Me. So I sent them away after their heart's fantasies, for following their own counsels. If only My people would hearken to Me, if Israel would go in My ways. In an instant I would subdue their enemies, and turn My hand against their tormentors. Those who hate the Lord would lie to

Him, so their destiny will be forever. But He would feed him with the finest of wheat, and satisfy you with honey from a rock.

Friday: Psalm 93
The Lord reigns; He is clothed with grandeur; the Lord has clothed and girded Himself with might; He also established the world firmly that it shall not falter. Your throne is established from of old; You are eternal. The rivers have raised, O Lord, the rivers have raised their voice; the rivers have raised their raging waves. More than the sound of many waters, mightier than the waves of the sea, the Lord is mighty on high. Your testimonies are most trustworthy; Your House will be resplendent in holiness, O Lord, forever.

Saturday: Psalm 92
*(This Psalm is a prophetic description
of the future Messianic Era.)*

A Psalm, a song for the seventh day. It is good to thank the Lord, and to sing praise to Your Name, O Most High. To proclaim Your kindness in the morning, and Your faithfulness in the nights, with a ten-stringed instrument and with a lyre, with singing accompanied by a harp. For You, Lord, have made me happy with Your deeds; I sing for joy at the works of Your hand. How great are Your works, O Lord! Your thoughts are exceedingly profound. A boor cannot know, and a fool cannot understand this: when the wicked thrive like grass, and all evildoers flourish, it is in order that they may be destroyed forever. But You, Lord, are exalted forever. Indeed, Your enemies, O Lord, indeed Your enemies will perish; all evildoers will be scattered. But You will increase my might like that of a wild ox; I will be anointed with fresh oil. My eyes have seen my watchful enemies; when evildoers rise up against me, my ears have heard. The righteous will flourish like a date palm; he will grow tall like a cedar in Lebanon. Planted in the House of the Lord, they will flourish in the court-yards of our God. They will still be fruitful in old age; they will be vigorous and fresh – to declare that the Lord is just; He is my strength, in Whom there is no injustice.

Individuals who are on a trip away from their home town may say the "Prayer for Travelers" on p. 75.

END OF MORNING SERVICE

AFTERNOON SERVICE

Leader: The Lord of hosts is with us; the God of Jacob is our stronghold forever.[41] Lord of hosts, happy is the man who trusts in You.[42] Lord, deliver us; may the King answer us on the day we call![43]

All recite Psalm 145:

A Psalm of praise by David: I will exalt You, my God the King, and bless Your Name forever. Every day I will bless You, and extol Your Name forever. The Lord is great and exceedingly exalted; there is no limit to His greatness. One generation to another will laud Your works, and tell of Your mighty acts. I will speak of the splendor of Your glorious majesty and of Your wondrous deeds. They will proclaim the might of Your awesome acts, and I will recount Your greatness. They will express the remembrance of Your abounding goodness, and sing of Your righteousness. The Lord is gracious and compassionate, slow to anger and of great kindness. The Lord is good to all, and His mercies extend over all His works. Lord, all Your works will give thanks to You, and Your pious ones will bless You. They will

---

[41] Psalms 46:8.
[42] Ibid. 84.13.
[43] Ibid. 20:10.

declare the glory of Your kingdom, and tell of Your strength, to make known to mankind His mighty acts, and the glorious majesty of His kingdom. Your kingship is a kingship over all worlds, and Your dominion is throughout all generations. The Lord supports all who fall, and straightens all who are bent. The eyes of all look expectantly to You, and You give them their food at the proper time. You open Your hand and satisfy the desire of every living thing. The Lord is righteous in all His ways, and benevolent in all His deeds. The Lord is close to all who call upon Him, to all who call upon Him in truth. He fulfills the desire of those who fear Him, hears their cry, and delivers them. The Lord watches over all who love Him, and will destroy all the wicked. My mouth will utter the praise of the Lord, and let all flesh bless His holy Name forever.

Group Torah Study (optional)[44]

Recite before the study begins:

For from Zion shall go forth the Torah, and the word of the Lord from Jerusalem. Blessed is He Who in His holiness gave the Torah to His people Israel. Blessed is the Name of the Master of the

---

[44] The halachic guidelines for Torah study by Noahides are published in *The Divine Code*, Part I, ch. 5, by Rabbi Moshe Weiner.

42

Universe! I do not put my trust in man, nor do I place my reliance on an angel, but only in the God of Heaven Who is the true God, Whose Torah is truth, Whose prophets are true, and Who performs numerous deeds of goodness and truth. I put my trust in Him, and I utter praises to His holy and glorious Name.[45]

Group Torah-Study Session (*sitting*)

Recite after the group study is concluded:

The Torah which Moses placed before the Children of Israel is a tree of life for those who hold fast to it, and those who support it are fortunate.[32] Its ways are pleasant ways, and all its paths are peace.[46] Who is the man who desires life, who loves long life wherein to see goodness? Guard your tongue from evil, and your lips from speaking deceitfully. Turn from evil and do good, seek peace and pursue it.[47]

---

[45] Cf. traditional *Siddur* prayer-book liturgy.
[46] Proverbs 3:17.
[47] Psalms 34:13-15.

"Amidah" (Standing) Prayer [48]

All recite quietly and devoutly, without interruptions:

Blessed are You, God, the Supreme Being Who bestows abundant kindness.

Please endow us graciously with wisdom, understanding, and knowledge.

Please accept our repentance, and forgive us for our errors and sins.

Grant complete healing for all our wounds and ailments.

Bestow upon us all the needs for our sustenance from Your bounty.

Hasten the day of which it is said: "God will be King over the entire earth; in that day God will be One and His Name One;"[49] "For then I will turn the peoples to pure language, so that all will call upon the Name of God to serve Him with one purpose;"[50] and "They will not harm or destroy on all My holy mountain, for the earth will be filled with knowledge of God as water covering the sea bed."[51]

Hear our voice, God, our merciful Father, have compassion upon us and accept our prayers in mercy and favor. *(Other requests may be inserted here.)* Blessed are You, God, who hears prayer.

---

[48] Composed for Noahides by Rabbi J. Immanuel Schochet.
[49] Zechariah 14:9.
[50] Zephaniah 3:9.
[51] Isaiah 11:9.

All assembled say the "Prayer of the Repentant"
(optional for an individual who prays alone)

O God, I have erred, sinned and willfully transgressed before You, and I have done that which is evil in Your eyes, especially with the sin(s) of … *(quietly state the specific sins or errors).*

I am sincerely ashamed of my sins, and I repent and firmly undertake not to do so again.

Please God, in Your infinite grace and compassion, forgive my sins and transgressions and grant me atonement, as it is written: "Let the wicked abandon his way and the man of iniquity his thoughts; and let him return unto God, and He will show him compassion, and to our God, for He will pardon abundantly."[52] And it is written: "Do I desire at all that the wicked should die, says the Lord, God; it is rather that he return from his ways and live!"[53]

---

[52] Isaiah 55:7.
[53] Ezekiel 18:23.

All recite the following prayer[54]

(Bow while saying "We bend the knee".)

We bend the knee, bow down, and offer praise, before the supreme King of kings, the Holy One blessed be He, Who stretches forth the Heavens and establishes the earth, the seat of whose glory is in the Heavens above, and the abode of Whose majesty is in the loftiest heights. He is our God; there is none else. Truly, He is our King; there is nothing besides Him, as it is written in His Torah: "Know this day and take unto your heart that the Lord is God; in the Heavens above and upon the earth below there is nothing else."[55]

And therefore we hope to You, Lord our God, that we may speedily behold the splendor of Your might, to banish idolatry from the earth – and false gods will be utterly destroyed; to perfect the world under the sovereignty of the Almighty. All mankind shall invoke Your Name, to turn to You all the wicked of the earth. Then all the inhabitants of the world will recognize and know that every knee should bend to You, every tongue should swear by Your Name. Before You, Lord our God, they will bow and prostrate themselves, and give honor to the glory of Your Name; and they will all take upon

---

[54] Cf. traditional *Siddur* prayer-book liturgy.
[55] Deuteronomy 4:39.

themselves the yoke of Your kingdom. May You soon reign over them forever and ever, for kingship is Yours, and to all eternity You will reign in glory, as it is written in Your Torah: "The Lord will reign forever and ever."[56] And it is said: "The Lord shall be King over the entire earth; on that day the Lord shall be One and His Name One."[57]

All recite:

Indeed, the righteous will extol Your Name; the upright will dwell in Your Presence.[58]

END OF AFTERNOON SERVICE

---

[56] Exodus 15:18.
[57] Zechariah 14:9.
[58] Psalms 140:14.

EVENING SERVICE

(WITH ADDITIONS FOR FRIDAY EVENING)

On Friday evening all may begin with reciting the following Psalms 92, 93 and 96.

Then, as on other nights, continue on p. 50.

Psalm 92:

A Psalm, a song for the seventh day. It is good to thank the Lord, and to sing praise to Your Name, O Most High. To proclaim Your kindness in the morning, and Your faithfulness in the nights, with a ten-stringed instrument and with a lyre, with singing accompanied by a harp. For You, Lord, have made me happy with Your deeds; I sing for joy at the works of Your hand. How great are Your works, O Lord! Your thoughts are exceedingly profound. A boor cannot know, and a fool cannot understand this: when the wicked thrive like grass, and all evildoers flourish, it is in order that they may be destroyed forever. But You, Lord, are exalted forever. Indeed, Your enemies, O Lord, indeed Your enemies will perish; all evildoers will be scattered. But You will increase my might like that of a wild ox; I will be anointed with fresh oil. My eyes have seen my watchful enemies; when evildoers rise up against me, my ears have heard. The righteous will flourish like a date palm; he will grow tall like a cedar in Lebanon. Planted in the House of the Lord, they will flourish in the courtyards of our God. They will still be fruitful in old age; they will be vigorous and fresh – to declare that the Lord is just; He is my strength, in Whom there is no injustice.

Psalm 93:

The Lord reigns; He is clothed with grandeur; the Lord has clothed and girded Himself with might; He also established the world firmly that it shall not falter. Your throne is established from of old; You are eternal. The rivers have raised, O Lord, the rivers have raised their voice; the rivers have raised their raging waves. More than the sound of many waters, mightier than the waves of the sea, the Lord is mighty on high. Your testimonies are most trustworthy; Your House will be resplendent in holiness, O Lord, forever.

Psalm 96:

Sing to the Lord a new song; sing to the Lord, everyone on earth. Sing to the Lord, bless His Name; proclaim His deliverance from day to day. Recount His glory among the nations, His wonders among all the peoples. For the Lord is great and highly praised; He is awesome above all gods. For all the gods of the nations are naught, but the Lord made the Heavens. Majesty and splendor are before Him, might and beauty in His sanctuary. Render to the Lord, O families of nations, render to the Lord honor and might. Render to the Lord honor due His Name; bring an offering and come to His courtyards. Bow down to the Lord in resplendent holiness; tremble before Him, everyone on earth. Proclaim among the nations: "The Lord reigns!" Indeed, the world is firmly established that it shall not falter. He will judge the peoples with righteousness. The Heavens will rejoice and the earth will rejoice; the sea and its fullness will roar; the fields and everything therein will exult; then all the trees of the forest will sing with joy – before the Lord, for He will have arrived, He will have arrived to judge the earth. He will judge the world with righteousness, and the nations with His truth.

On all nights, continue to recite here:

A Song of Ascents. Bless the Lord, all servants of the Lord, who stand in the house of the Lord at night. Raise your hands in holiness and bless the Lord. May the Lord, Maker of Heaven and earth, bless you from Zion.[59]

By day the Lord ordains His kindness, and at night His song is with me, a prayer to the God of my life![60] The deliverance of the righteous is from the Lord, their strength in time of distress. The Lord helps them and delivers them; He delivers them from the wicked and saves them, because they have put their trust in Him.[61]

Leader: Blessed, praised, glorified, exalted and upraised is the Name of the King Who rules over kings, the Holy One, Blessed is He, for He is the First and the Last, and aside from Him there is no other. His Name is exalted beyond every blessing and praise. Blessed is the Name of His glorious kingdom for all eternity. Blessed be the Name of the Lord, from this time and forever.[62]

---

[59] Psalm 134.
[60] Ibid. 42:9.
[61] Ibid. 37:39-40.
[62] Cf. traditional Ashkenazi *Siddur* prayer-book liturgy.

All stand while the Leader chants:

Bless the Lord Who is blessed.

*All respond***:** Blessed be the Lord Who is blessed for all eternity.

Meditation: As Noahides, when we accept and follow the ways of God based on Torah with the faithful of Israel as our guides, we link our destiny to theirs. It is appropriate to confirm this solidarity by verbally accepting God's Unity and Kingship:

Accepting God's Unity and Kingship:[63]

Almighty God, we accept upon ourselves that which is written in Your Torah: "You shall know this day and take to your heart that God [alone] is God, in the Heavens above and on the earth below – there is none other!"[64]

We affirm the precepts of "You shall love God, your God, with all your heart, and all your soul, and all your might" and "Fear the Lord, your God, and serve Him, and in His Name [alone] shall you vow;"[65] and as it says, "Fear God and keep His commandments, for that is a person's entire duty."[66]

---

[63] This and the following "Amidah" prayer were composed by Rabbi J. I. Schochet.
[64] Deuteronomy 4:39.
[65] Ibid. 6:5,13
[66] Ecclesiastes 12:13.

"Amidah" (Standing) Prayer

All recite quietly and devoutly, without interruptions:

Blessed are You, God, the Supreme Being who bestows abundant kindness.

Please endow us graciously with wisdom, understanding, and knowledge.

Please accept our repentance, and forgive us for our errors and sins.

Grant complete healing for all our wounds and ailments.

Bestow upon us all the needs for our sustenance from Your bounty.

Hasten the day of which it is said: "God will be King over the entire earth; in that day God will be One and His Name One;"[67] "For then I will turn the peoples to pure language, so that all will call upon the Name of God to serve Him with one purpose;"[68] and "They will not harm or destroy on all My holy mountain, for the earth will be filled with knowledge of God as water covering the sea bed."[69] Hear our voice, God, our merciful Father, have compassion upon us and accept our prayers in mercy and favor. *(Other requests may be inserted here.)* Blessed are You, God, who hears prayer.

---

[67] Zechariah 14:9.

[68] Zephaniah 3:9.

[69] Isaiah 11:9.

All recite the following prayer [70]

(Bow while saying "We bend the knee".)

We bend the knee, bow down, and offer praise, before the supreme King of kings, the Holy One blessed be He, Who stretches forth the Heavens and establishes the earth, the seat of whose glory is in the heavens above, and the abode of Whose majesty is in the loftiest heights. He is our God; there is none else. Truly, He is our King; there is nothing besides Him, as it is written in His Torah: "Know this day and take unto your heart that the Lord is God; in the Heavens above and upon the earth below there is nothing else."[71]

And therefore we hope to You, Lord our God, that we may speedily behold the splendor of your might, to banish idolatry from the earth –and false gods will be utterly destroyed; to perfect the world under the sovereignty of the Almighty. All mankind shall invoke Your Name, to turn to You all the wicked of the earth. Then all the inhabitants of the world will recognize and know that every knee should bend to You, every tongue should swear by Your Name. Before You, Lord our God, they will bow and prostrate themselves, and give honor to the glory of Your Name; and they will all take upon

---

[70] Cf. traditional *Siddur* prayer-book liturgy.
[71] Deuteronomy 4:39.

themselves the yoke of Your kingdom. May You soon reign over them forever and ever, for kingship is Yours, and to all eternity You will reign in glory, as it is written in Your Torah: "The Lord will reign forever and ever."[72] And it is said: "The Lord shall be King over the entire earth; on that day the Lord shall be One and His Name One."[73]

All recite:

Indeed, the righteous will extol Your Name; the upright will dwell in Your Presence.[74]

END OF THE EVENING SERVICE

We go home in peace.

---

[72] Exodus 15:18.
[73] Zechariah 14:9.
[74] Psalms 140:14.

Evening Prayers Before Sleeping

These prayers are recited by the individual.

Psalm 91:

Whoever dwells in the shelter of the Most High, who abides in the shadow of the Almighty: I say of the Lord who is my refuge and my stronghold, my God in whom I trust, that He will save you from the ensnaring trap, from the destructive pestilence. He will cover you with His pinion, and you will find refuge under His wings; His truth is a shield and an armor. You will not fear the terror of the night, nor the arrow that flies by day, nor the pestilence that prowls in the darkness, nor the destruction that ravages at noon. A thousand may fall at your side, and ten thousand at your right, but it shall not reach you. You need only look with your eyes, and you will see the retribution of the wicked. Because you [have said,] "The Lord is my shelter," and you have made the Most High your haven, no evil will befall you, no plague will come near your tent. For He will instruct His angels in your behalf, to guard you in all your ways. They will carry you in their hands, lest you injure your foot upon a rock. You will tread upon the lion and the viper; you will trample upon the young lion and the serpent. Because he desires Me, I will deliver him; I will fortify him, for he knows My Name. When he calls on Me, I will answer him; I am with him in distress. I will deliver him and honor him. I will satisfy him with long life, and show him My deliverance

Psalm 121:
A song of Ascents. I lift my eyes to the mountains; from where will my help come? My help will come from the Lord, Maker of Heaven and earth. He will not let your foot falter; your Guardian does not slumber. Indeed, the Guardian of Israel neither slumbers nor sleeps. The Lord is your Guardian; the Lord is your protective shade at your right hand. The sun will not harm you by day, nor the moon by night. The Lord will guard you from all evil; He will guard your soul. The Lord will guard your going and your coming, from now and for all time.

Lord of the universe, Who reigned before anything was created – at the time when He made all by His will, then was His Name proclaimed King. And after all things will be uplifted, the Awesome One will reign alone. He was, He is, and He shall be in glory. He is One, and there is no other to compare to Him, to call His equal. Without beginning, without end – power and dominion belong to Him. He is my God and my ever-living Redeemer, the strength of my lot in time of distress. He is my banner and my refuge, my portion on the day I call.

Into His hand I entrust my spirit when I sleep and when I wake. And with my soul, my body too, the Lord is with me, I shall not fear.[75]

Prayer of the Repentant [76]

An individual may say this at any appropriate time.

O God, I have erred, sinned, and willfully transgressed before You, and I have done that which is evil in Your eyes, especially with the sin(s) of ... (*state the specific sins or errors*).

I am sincerely ashamed of my sins, and I repent and firmly undertake not to do so again. Please God, in Your infinite grace and compassion forgive my sins and transgressions and grant me atonement, as it is written: "Let the wicked abandon his way and the man of iniquity his thoughts; and let him return unto God, and He will show him compassion, and to our God, for He will pardon abundantly." [77] And it is written: "Do I desire at all that the wicked should die, says the Lord, God; it is rather that he return from his ways and live!" [78]

---

[75] The *"Adon Olom"* prayer from the traditional *Siddur* prayer-book liturgy.

[76] This prayer was composed by Rabbi J. Immanuel Schochet.

[77] Isaiah 55:7.

[78] Ezekiel 18:23.

Psalm 51:

For the choirmaster, a Psalm by David, when Nathan the prophet came to him after he had gone to Bathsheba. Be gracious to me, O God, in keeping with Your kindness; in accordance with Your abounding compassion, erase my transgressions. Cleanse me thoroughly of my wrongdoing, and purify me of my sin. For I acknowledge my transgressions, and my sin is always before me. Against You alone have I sinned, and done that which is evil in Your eyes; [forgive me] so that You will be justified in Your verdict, vindicated in Your judgment. Indeed, I was begotten in iniquity, and in sin did my mother conceive me. Indeed, You desire truth in the innermost parts; teach me the wisdom of concealed things. Purge me with hyssop and I shall be pure; cleanse me and I shall be whiter than snow. Let me hear joy and gladness; then the bones that You have shattered will rejoice. Hide Your face from my sins, and erase all my trespasses. Create in me a pure heart, O God, and renew within me an upright spirit. Do not cast me out from before You, and do not take Your Spirit of Holiness away from me. Restore to me the joy of Your deliverance, and support me with a spirit of generosity. I will teach transgressors Your ways, and sinners will return to You. Save me from bloodguilt, O God, God of my deliverance; my tongue will sing joyously of Your righteousness. My Lord, open my lips, and my mouth shall declare Your praise. For You do not desire that I bring sacrifices, nor do You wish burnt offerings. The offering [desirable] to God is a contrite spirit; a contrite and broken heart, God, You do not disdain. In Your goodwill, bestow goodness upon Zion; rebuild the walls of Jerusalem. Then You will desire offerings of righteousness, burnt-offering and whole-offering; then they will offer bulls upon Your altar.

One may recite other verses of Psalms,
with introspection.

Recite the following:

When you lie down, you will not be afraid; you will lie down, and your sleep will be sweet.[79]

May I sleep well; may I awake in mercy.[80]

I entrust my spirit into Your hand; You will redeem me God, God of truth![81]

---

[79] Proverbs 3:24.
[80] From the traditional *Siddur* prayer-book liturgy.
[81] Psalms 31:6.

FRIDAY EVENING IN THE HOME

On Friday after sundown, one or more members of the home may light one or more candles on the dinner table (without a blessing), to beautify the family's evening meal. This may be delegated to the women and girls of the home. The following prayers may be said either after lighting the candles, or before starting the meal, or as a conclusion to the prayer of "Grace After a Meal," p. 71:

May it be Your will, Lord our God, that the light of Your commandments will enlighten the whole world, that all who come into the world will unite with their part in Your Torah, and that Your Temple be rebuilt soon in our time, so that we may serve You there reverently.

May it be Your will, Lord our God, Creator of the Universe and God of all humanity, that You show favor to all Your servants, and in particular to me and my family, and that You grant us long life in service to You, that You remember us with beneficent remembrance and blessing, that You consider us with a consideration of salvation and compassion, that You bless us with great blessing, that You make our household complete, and that You cause Your Presence to enlighten us.

May it be Your will, Lord our God, to privilege us to raise children and grandchildren who are wise and understanding, who love and fear You, that they may grow up to be people of truth who are attached to You, that they may illuminate the world with good and righteous deeds, and that their labors be in service of You, God, Creator of the Universe.

Please hear our supplications at this time, and let Your kind attention shine upon us.

BLESSINGS FOR FAMILY MEMBERS

These prayers and blessings may be said before a special meal, or on any special occasions.

Blessing one's children

Parent places hands on the child's head and recites:

May God Almighty, Maker of Heaven and earth, bless you, *(say the child's given names)*, to walk humbly with Him among the righteous of the nations. May the Almighty watch over you, shine His face toward you, show you favor, and grant you peace, both now and forever more.

The child responds: Amen.

A man may recite the following in honor of his wife. Anyone may recite this in honor of their mother or grandmother:

A Woman of Valor

(Proverbs 31:10-31)

Who can find a woman of valor? Her value far exceeds that of gems. Her husband relies on her, and he lacks no gain. She treats him with goodness and not with evil, all the days of her life. She seeks wool and flax, and she works willingly with her hands. She is like the merchant ships; she brings her food from afar. She rises when it is still night; she gives food to her household and sets out the tasks for her maids. She considers a field and buys it; from her earnings she plants a vineyard. She girds her loins with strength and flexes her arms. She realizes that her enterprise is profitable; her lamp does not go out at night. She stretches forth her hands onto the distaff, and her hands support the spindle. She spreads out her hand to the poor, and she stretches her hands out to the needy. She does not fear for her household in the frost, for all her household are dressed in crimson. She makes her own tapestries; her garments are fine linen and purple. Her husband is well-known at the gates, as he sits with the elders of the land. She makes linens and sells them, and she provides belts to the merchants. She is clothed in strength and beauty, and she looks smilingly toward the future. She opens her mouth with wisdom, and the teaching of kindness is on her tongue. She supervises the ways of her household and does not eat the bread of idleness. Her children rise and praise her; [also] her husband, and he praises her: "Many daughters have done worthily, but you surpass them all." Charm is deceptive and beauty is naught; a God-fearing woman is the one to be praised. Give her praise for her accomplishments, and let her deeds praise her at the gates.

BLESSINGS BEFORE EATING OR DRINKING

Before a person eats or drinks, it is proper to say words of praise and blessing to God, as thanks for that which God has provided for his needs and enjoyment.

Recommended versions of the traditional blessings before eating or drinking are given here. These six blessings correspond to the various categories of food. (Upon hearing these specific blessings said to God by others, it is correct to respond "Amen".)

i. Before eating bread:

Blessed are You, Lord our God, King of the universe, Who brings forth bread from the earth.[82]

Examples: bread, bagels, pita bread, and rolls – if the flour is from wheat, barley, rye, oats or spelt, mixed with water as the main liquid.

ii. Before eating other cooked foods made from grain flour or rice:

Blessed are You, Lord our God, King of the universe, Who creates various kinds of sustenance.

---

[82] Cf. Psalms 104:14.

Examples: cakes, cereals, cookies, crackers, pasta, pastries, cream of wheat, cooked rice, rice cakes (and unleavened bread if it is eaten as a snack).

iii. Before drinking grape wine or grape juice:

Blessed are You, Lord our God, King of the universe, Who creates the fruit of the vine.

iv. Before eating fruit of a tree:

Blessed are You, Lord our God, King of the universe, Who creates the fruit of the tree.

Examples: fruit of *perennial* trees, bushes, cacti and woody vines, such as apples, blueberries, cranberries, grapes, kiwi fruit, and nuts (except peanut, which is a root).

v. Before eating produce of other plants:

Blessed are You, Lord our God, King of the universe. Who creates the fruit of the earth.

Examples: edible roots (e.g. peanuts), leafy greens, vegetables (e.g. tomatoes, legumes), and annual or perennial herbaceous fruit (e.g. bananas, artichokes, strawberries, pineapples, melons).

vi. Before any other type of food or beverage:

(Use this blessing if in doubt as to which one of the above blessings applies.)

Blessed are You, Lord our God, King of the universe, by Whose word all things came to be.

***Examples*:** dairy products, eggs, meats, fish, mushrooms, fully processed foods (e.g. smooth peanut butter, tofu, candy), beverages (except grape wine or grape juice), and any type of food not included in the examples above.

RULES OF BLESSING BEFORE EATING OR DRINKING

1. A blessing may be said even if only a small amount of food or beverage will be consumed.

2. Before beginning to recite one of the listed blessings (i) - (vi) for a food, one should know which one is the correct blessing to say.

3. After beginning to recite a blessing, do not interrupt with other words until the first bite or drink is swallowed.

4. Since names of God are part of the blessings, and it is forbidden to say God's names in vain, one should only say them under the necessary conditions. (When teaching them to a child, one may pronounce God's name if needed, until the child has learned the words.)

5. One should answer "Amen" immediately after hearing a blessing made by another person, if he is sure that the person is blessing only God. (But one does not conclude with "Amen" after his own blessing.)

6. If several different foods in the same category will be eaten, say only one blessing that will cover all of them. For example, when eating apples and oranges, say the blessing (iv) only once, and intend to include all the fruit.

7. When blessing (vi) is said for a food, then non-grape beverages that will be drunk are included as well.

8. If different categories of foods will be eaten without bread, the order of reciting blessings for each type of food is in the order of the blessings listed above. For example, when beginning to eat a mixed salad, first say the blessing for avocado [blessing (iv), thus including all fruits], then for lettuce [blessing (v), thus including all vegetables], and then for cheese [blessing (vi), thus including all other types of food].

9. For a dish that contains a primary food mixed together with secondary foods of different types, only the blessing for the primary food is said. For example, say only blessing (i) for raisin bread, and only blessing (ii) for apple pie.

10. If the correct specific blessing is not known, in doubt or forgotten, blessing (vi) can be said to cover any food or drink.

11. When starting a meal with the blessing for bread, the blessing (i) can cover the entire meal (since all foods are secondary to bread), so blessings are not said for the other foods or drinks. (But grape wine or grape juice always receives its own blessing, even during a meal with bread.)

12. After saying the blessing over grape wine or grape juice, an additional blessing for any other beverages is not necessary, since all other beverages are secondary.

OTHER BLESSINGS

When smelling sweet spices such as cloves or cinnamon:

Blessed are You, Lord our God, King of the universe, Who creates various kinds of spices.

On hearing news or experiencing an event that is good for both oneself and others:

Blessed are You, Lord our God, King of the universe, Who is good and does good.

After a miracle occurs for a person, if he returns to that place after an interval of a month or more, he may recite:

Blessed are You, Lord our God, King of the universe, Who performed a miracle for me in this place.

If miracles were also done for you in other places, include those by saying:

Blessed are You, Lord our God, King of the universe, Who performed a miracle for me in this place, and in … [*such-and-such a place*].

GRACE AFTER A MEAL

After a person eats or drinks a satisfying amount, it is fitting for him to thank and bless God for giving him his sustenance. It is customary to recite a prayer of "Grace" after eating a filling meal, but not after eating only a small amount of food. When saying Grace after a meal, it is proper to include thanks to God for other necessities – for example, health, livelihood, and existence. The following two paragraphs are recommended:[83]

We offer thanks to You, Master of the universe, Who in His great goodness, provides sustenance for the entire world with grace, with kindness, and with mercy. He gives food to all flesh, for His kindness is everlasting.[84] Through His great goodness to us continuously, we do not lack food,[85] and may we never lack food, for the sake of His great Name. For He, benevolent God, provides nourishment and sustenance for all, does good to all, and prepares food for all His creatures whom He has created, as it is said: You open Your hand and satisfy the desire of every living thing.[86] Blessed is the God of the universe, from Whose bounty we have eaten.[87]

---

[83] Rabbi M. Weiner, *The Divine Code*, 3rd Ed., p. 86, pub. Ask Noah International.

[84] Psalms 136:25.

[85] Having just completed a meal.

[86] Psalms 145:16.

[87] From *Midrash Rabbah Genesis*, ch. 54.

Please, Master of the universe, in Your mercy give us life, health, livelihood, and sustenance, so that we may thank and bless You always. Please do not make us dependent upon the gifts of mortal men nor upon their loans, but only upon Your full, open, and generous hand, that we may never be shamed or disgraced. Give thanks to the Lord for He is good, for His kindness is everlasting.[88] Blessed is the man who trusts in the Lord, and the Lord will be his security.[89]

One may extend the Grace after a meal with further requests to God as desired.

Shorter option for Grace after a meal:

This is the blessing that was taught by Abraham to the guests who dined in his tent:[90]

Blessed is the God of the universe, from Whose bounty we have eaten.

---

[88] Psalms 136:1.

[89] Jeremiah 17:7.

[90] See footnote 87.

7 Verses for Noahide Children to Learn

Rabbi J. Immanuel Schochet recommended seven verses for Noahide children to learn to recite by heart and sing at bedtime. Parents and teachers may add other Hebrew Bible verses as they feel are appropriate.

1. *(Genesis 1:1)* In the beginning God created the Heavens and the earth.

2. *(Genesis 5:1)* On the day that God created Adam, He made him in the image of God.

3. *(Psalms 34:15)* Turn away from bad and do good; seek peace and pursue it.

4. *(Psalms 145:9)* The Lord is good to all, and His mercies extend over all His works.

5. *(Proverbs 15:3)* The eyes of the Lord are everywhere, seeing the bad and the good.

6. *(Job 28:28)* Behold, the fear of the Lord is wisdom, and turning away from bad is understanding.

7. *(Isaiah 48:17)* Thus said the Lord, your Redeemer, the Holy One of Israel: I am the Lord, your God, Who teaches you for your benefit, Who guides you in the way you should go.

PRAYERS FOR SPECIFIC NEEDS AND REQUESTS

A PRAYER FOR LIVELIHOOD[91]

May it be Your Will, Lord our God, that my provisions and my livelihood, and the provisions and livelihood of my household, be encompassing, appropriate and virtuous in Your hands. May we never be in need of the gifts of man nor of their loans, but only of Your hand which is full, open, holy, and generous. And may my work and all my dealings be blessed and not destitute, for life and not for death. And may I merit that no desecration of the Name of Heaven occur through me, and that I may be among the charitable and those that influence for good to everyone at all times, and fill my hand with Your blessings and satiate me of Your goodness. For You are blessed and bring blessings to the universe. The eyes of all look expectedly to You, and You give them all their food in its proper time. You open Your hand, and satisfy the desire of every living being. Cast your burden upon the Lord, and He will sustain you; He will never allow the falling of the righteous. Please lift my strength and raise my fortune in order that I will be able to serve You whole-heartedly all the days of the world. Amen.

---

[91] From the prayer by Rabbi Moshe Cordovero.

Prayer for Travelers[92]

This prayer is said outside the town from which one is leaving, on the first day of the journey. On subsequent days of the journey until reaching home again, the prayer may be recited every morning.

May it be Your will, Lord our God, to lead us in peace and direct our steps in peace, to guide us in peace, to support us in peace, and to bring us to our destination in life, joy, and peace

(if one intends to return on the same day, add:
and return us in peace).

Deliver us from the hands of every enemy and lurking foe, from robbers and wild beasts on the journey, and from all kinds of calamities that may come and afflict the world; and bestow blessing upon all our actions. Grant me grace, kindness, and mercy in Your eyes and in the eyes of all who behold us, and bestow bountiful kindness upon us. Hear the voice of our prayer, for You hear everyone's prayer. Blessed are You, God, Who hears prayer.

---

[92] From *Siddur Tehillat HaShem with English Translation, Annotated Edition*, p. 85, pub. Kehot.

PRAYER FOR A SICK PERSON

In addition to Psalm 20 below and any other Psalms said for the sick person, one may pray the following. Names of more than one person can be combined in one prayer.

For a male: May the Holy One, blessed be He, be filled with mercy for *(mention the sick person's given names)*, son of *(use* Noah *if the sick person is a Gentile; use* Sarah *if the sick person is a Jew)*, to restore him to health and to cure him, to strengthen him and to invigorate him. And may God hasten to send him from Heaven a complete recovery to all his bodily parts and veins, a healing of spirit and a healing of body. Amen.

For a female: May the Holy One, blessed be He, be filled with mercy for *(mention the sick person's given names)*, daughter of *(use* Noah *if the sick person is a Gentile; use* Sarah *if the sick person is a Jew)*, to restore her to health and to cure her, to strengthen her and to invigorate her. And may God hasten to send her from Heaven a complete recovery to all her bodily parts and veins, a healing of spirit and a healing of body. Amen.

It is appropriate to donate to a proper charity, and to do other acts of goodness and kindness, for the sake of the healing of the sick person.

PSALM 20

In any time of need, this Psalm is a prayer for help or healing, or delivery from trouble or difficulties. One should mention the name (as above) of the person who is being prayed for (even for oneself) and the help that is needed, and be strong in faith and trust in God. It is good to say the prayer and this Psalm along with making a donation for proper charity.

For the choirmaster, a Psalm by David. May the Lord answer you on the day of distress; may the Name of the God of Jacob fortify you. May He send your help from the Sanctuary, and support you from Zion. May He remember all your offerings, and always accept favorably your sacrifices. May He grant you your heart's desire, and fulfill your every plan. We will rejoice in your deliverance, and raise our banners in the Name of our God; may the Lord fulfill all your wishes. Now I know that the Lord has delivered His anointed one, answering him from His holy Heavens with the mighty saving power of His right hand. Some [rely] upon chariots and some upon horses, but we invoke the Name of the Lord our God. They bend and fall, but we rise and are invigorated. Lord, deliver us; may the King answer us on the day we call.

PRAYER FOR A NEWBORN GENTILE BABY

For a baby boy:

May God bless the woman who has given birth, (*mention her full name*) daughter of Noah, together with the child born to her, (*mention the baby's full name*) son of Noah. May he be brought up by his parents to the Seven Laws of Noah, wholesome marriage and good deeds.

For a baby girl:

May God bless the woman who has given birth, (*mention her full name*) daughter of Noah, together with the child born to her, (*mention the baby's full name*) daughter of Noah. May she be brought up by her parents to the Seven Laws of Noah, wholesome marriage and good deeds.

On any day, one may recite a child's or adult's "chapter of Psalms" in prayer for the person's well-being. The person's "chapter of Psalms" is the chapter number that equals the person's age + 1. (the person's age on the next birthday).

PRAYER FOR A DEPARTED SOUL[93]

All or part of the following prayer may be recited (not more than once daily) during a funeral or memorial gathering, the week of mourning, an anniversary of passing, or other special occasions that are deemed appropriate.

May God remember the soul of (*mention the deceased person's given names*), son/daughter of (*use* Noah *if the deceased is a Gentile; use* Abraham *if the deceased is a Jew*), who has gone on to his/her world. By virtue of my praying on his/her behalf, and, without making a vow, my intent to donate proper charity on his/her behalf, may his/her soul be bound in the Bond of Life together with the souls of the righteous, and let us say: Amen.

Only respectable behavior should take place in the presence of the deceased or in a funeral home or cemetery. Discussions should focus on the good personal qualities of the deceased, or on funeral arrangements. In addition to the above prayer, the following Psalms may be recited. by the mourners or eulogist as meditations on earthly life.

---

[93] This prayer was composed by Rabbi J. Immanuel ˙Schochet.

Psalms that May be Recited by Mourners

All or part of the following Psalms may be recited by the mourners or eulogist as meditations on earthly life.

Psalm 23:

A Psalm by David. The Lord is my Shepherd; I shall lack nothing. He lays me down in green pastures; He leads me beside still waters. He revives my soul; He directs me on paths of righteousness for the sake of His name. Though I walk through the valley of the shadow of death, I fear no evil, for You are with me; Your rod and Your staff – they will comfort me. You will prepare for me before my enemies; You have anointed my head with oil; my cup is full. Only goodness and kindness shall follow me all the days of my life, and I shall dwell in the House of the Lord for many long years.

Psalm 49:1-10,16-19

For the Conductor, by the sons of Korach, a Psalm. Hear this all you peoples; listen, all you inhabitants of the world; sons of common folk and sons of nobility, rich and poor alike. My mouth speaks wisdom, and the thoughts of my heart are understanding. I incline my ear to the parable; I will unravel my riddle upon the harp. Why should I be afraid in times of trouble? [Because] the sins of my heels surround me. There are those who rely on their wealth, who boast of their great riches. Yet a man cannot redeem his brother, nor pay his ransom to God. The ransom of their soul is too costly, and forever unattainable. Can one live forever, never to see the grave? But God will redeem my soul from the hands of the grave, for He will take me, *Selah*. Do not fear when a man grows rich, when the glory of his house is increased; for when he dies he will take nothing, his glory will not descend after him. For he [alone] praises himself in his lifetime; but [all] will praise you if you better yourself.

Psalms 139:1-18

For the Conductor, by David, a Psalm. O Lord, You have probed me, and You know. You know my sitting down and my standing up; You perceive my thought from afar. You encircle my going about and my lying down; You are familiar with all my paths. For there was not yet a word on my tongue – and behold, Lord, You knew it all. Back and front You have restricted me, and you have laid Your hand upon me. Knowledge [to escape You] is beyond me; it is exalted, I cannot know it. Where can I go [away] from Your spirit? And where can I flee from

Your Presence? If I ascend to the Heavens, You are there; if I make my bed in the grave, behold, You are there. Were I to take up wings as the dawn and dwell in the furthest part of the sea, there, too, Your hand would guide me; Your right hand would hold me. Were I to say, "Surely the darkness will shadow me," then the night would be as light around me. Even the darkness obscures nothing from You; and the night shines like the day – the darkness is as light. For You created my mind; You covered me in my mother's womb. I will thank You, for I was formed in an awesome and wondrous way; unfathomable are Your works, though my soul perceived much. My essence was not hidden from You even while I was born in concealment, formed in the lowest parts of the earth. Your eyes saw my unshaped form, and all were recorded in Your book, even those to be formed in future days – to Him they are the same. How precious are Your thoughts to me, O God! How overwhelming are their beginnings! Were I to count them, they would outnumber the sand, even if I were to remain awake and always with You.

COMMEMORATING THE ANNIVERSARY
OF A PERSON'S PASSING

It is appropriate to light a candle on that date in remembrance of the person's soul. It is preferable to light a candle that will burn for the entire 24 hours, on the secular date for a Gentile, and on the date in the Hebrew calendar for a Jew.

From the teachings of the Lubavitcher Rebbe:[94]

This anniversary is marked in many societies and is relevant and comprehensible to all people. The good aspect of the day is that the surviving relatives ought to become inspired to undertake good resolutions and increase in good deeds, and influence positively those around them, anywhere that they can reach. This will also increase one's joy in doing good deeds in the memory of the loved one. Like all aspects of one's Divine service, this ought to be with joy and inner gladness. When the date comes around annually, it causes "the living to take to heart," i.e., one is inspired to repent, increase in charity and behave in a pleasant, peaceful manner. The underlying purpose is to make recognizable to the entire world that God "formed it for dwelling." [95]

---

[94] *Hisvaaduyos* 5747, Vol. 2, p. 407.
[95] From Isaiah 45:18.

PSALMS AND PRAYERS FOR ELUL, TISHREI, ROSH HASHANAH AND HANUKAH

Additional Daily Psalms from First of Elul through End of Sukkot (Hoshanah Rabbah)

There is a custom for Jews to recite three Psalms per day, beginning with the first day of Elul (Psalms 1-3 on day 1, Psalms 4-6 on day 2, etc.), through Psalm 114 on the ninth of Tishrei, which is the Eve of Yom Kippur. Then groups of nine Psalms are recited at four times during Yom Kippur, until the final Psalm 150 is concluded at the end of the day.

Rabbi Moshe Weiner has said that it is also a very good idea for Noahides to do this, either as above until the end of Yom Kippur, or continuing to recite three Psalms per day so that the final Psalm 150 is completed on the last day of Sukkot (called Hoshanah Rabbah). It is logical for Noahides to choose the option to keep the recitation at three Psalms per day so it extends through Sukkot, because the seven days of Sukkot are the time during the year when God judges the nations of the world for the amount of rain each one will receive. Also, during the times of the First and Second Holy Temples, those were the days when a total of 70 special sacrifices were brought, and they were offered on behalf of the nations of the world (of which there were 70 in Biblical times).

The schedule for saying three chapters of Psalms per day through the end of Sukkot is listed below. (Whoever did not start on the first day of Elul should begin with the Psalms of the particular day on which he starts the recitation, and complete the missing Psalms later.)

For the Month of Elul

Day	Psalms	Day	Psalms
1	1 – 3	16	46 – 48
2	4 – 6	17	49 – 51
3	7 – 9	18	52 – 54
4	10 – 12	19	55 – 57
5	13 – 15	20	58 – 60
6	16 – 18	21	61 – 63
7	19 – 21	22	64 – 66
8	22 – 24	23	67 – 69
9	25 – 27	24	70 – 72
10	28 – 30	25	73 – 75
11	31 – 33	26	76 – 78
12	34 – 36	27	79 – 81
13	37 – 39	28	82 – 84
14	40 – 42	29	85 – 87
15	43 – 45		

For the Month of Tishrei

Day	Psalms
1	88 – 90*
2	91 – 93
3	94 – 96
4	97 – 99
5	100 – 102
6	103 – 105
7	106 – 108
8	109 – 111
9	112 – 114
10	115 – 117**
11	118 – 120
12	121 – 123
13	124 – 126
14	127 – 129
15	130 – 132***
16	133 – 135
17	136 – 138
18	139 – 141
19	142 – 144
20	145 – 147
21	148 – 150

*Rosh Hashanah (first day)

**Yom Kippur

***First Day of Sukkot

Blessing One's Gentile Children on the Eve of Rosh Hashanah

Fathers and mothers may bless their children, that they be inscribed and sealed by God in the Book of Life, to have goodness and fear of God. The parent places hands on the child's head, speaks heartfelt blessings, and then recites the following prayer:

May it be the will of our Father in Heaven to place into your heart love and fear of Him. May the fear of God be upon you always so that you never sin. May your yearnings be for the Torah and its Seven Noahide Laws. May your eyes look in the straight way, may your mouth speak wisdom, and may your heart feel awe for God. May your hands engage in deeds of goodness and kindness, and may your feet run to fulfill the will of your Father in Heaven. May He grant you children who are righteous, who will be engaged in study and observance of their commandments throughout their lives. May your livelihood be blessed, and may your sustenance be earned in a permitted manner, with ease and bounty from God's generous hand, rather than from the gifts of flesh and blood, with sustenance that will give you easy opportunity for the service of God. May God count you among the righteous and pious God fearing people of the world. Amen!

ADDITIONS FOR EVENING AND MORNING SERVICES
ON THE FIRST DAY OF ROSH HASHANAH

*In the **Evening Service**, after concluding the "Amidah" prayer on p. 52, insert the recitation of Psalm 24 (the Psalm of the Day for Sunday, p. 33). Each verse is repeated out loud after the Leader.*

*In the **Morning Service**, insert the following prayers with the theme of God's Kingship, after Psalm 20 on p. 30.*

[O God,] Your Kingship is exalted, Your throne is established with lovingkindness, and You are seated on it in truth. It is true that You are the Judge, the One who presents evidence, the Knower and the Witness, who records and seals, who counts and reckons, and You remember all things that are forgotten. You open the Book of Remembrance and it reads itself; every person's signature is in it... All created beings pass before You, [one by one,] like a flock of sheep. As a shepherd examines his flock, so do You cause to pass [before You] every living soul, and You count, reckon and are mindful of [them], and You allocate the fixed portion for the needs of all Your creatures, and inscribe the verdict of their judgment.

But [a person's] repentance, prayer and charity avert the strictness of the decree!

For as is Your Name so is Your praise. You are slow to anger and easy to pacify, for You do not desire the death of one deserving death, but that he return from his [sinful] path and live. And [even] until the day of his death You wait for him; if he will but repent, You will welcome him at once. Truly, You are their Creator and You know their evil inclination, for they are but flesh and blood. A person's origin is dust and his end is unto dust. He earns his bread at the risk of his life. He is likened to a broken potsherd, to withering grass, to a fading flower, to a passing shadow, to a vanishing cloud, to a blowing wind, to dust that scatters and to a fleeting dream.

But You are the King, the living and eternal God![96]

---

[96] Based on the translation in the Rosh HaShanah prayer book, *Machzor HaShalem,* published by Kehot, 19'83.

Reciting the beliefs of the faithful:[97]

He is the faithful God.

He probes and He searches hidden secrets.

He probes man's thoughts.

He redeems from death and delivers from the grave.

He is the mighty Redeemer.

He alone judges all created beings.

He is the true Judge.

He is called "I will Be What I will Be."[98]

He was, He is, and He will be.

Sure is his Name, likewise His praise.

He is, and there is none beside Him.

He remembers with a favorable remembrance those who remember Him.

He remembers the Covenant.

He apportions life to all living beings.

He is eternal.

He is good and does good to the wicked and the good.

He is good to all.

He knows the inclination of creatures.

He has formed them in the womb.

He is all powerful and contains them all.

He is all-powerful.

He, the Omnipotent, abides in mystery, in shadow.

He is One Alone.

---

[97] Based on the Jewish prayer, "And all believe."

[98] Exodus 3:14.

He enthrones kings, and Kingship is His.

He is King of the world.

He guides every generation with lovingkindness.

He preserves kindness.

He is patient and He overlooks [the actions of] the rebellious.

He pardons forever.

He is the Most High, and His eye is directed to those who fear Him.

He answers silent [whispered] prayer.

He opens the gate for those who knock in repentance.

His hand is open. He waits for the evildoer, and desires that he be cleared of guilt.

He is righteous and upright.

His wrath is brief and He is forbearing.

He is hard to anger.

He is merciful and causes mercy to precede wrath.

He is easily appeased.

He is immutable, and treats small and great alike.

He is the righteous Judge. He is perfect and acts with perfection to those who are sincere.

His work is perfect!

[God,] You alone will be exalted and will reign over all in Oneness, as it is written: "On that day the Lord shall be One and His Name One!"[99]

---

[99] Zechariah 14:9.

PSALM 30 FOR HANUKAH

*It is appropriate to recite this Psalm on
any or all of the days or nights of Hanukah:*

A Psalm, a song of dedication of the Temple, by David. I exalt You, Lord, for You have uplifted me, and did not let my enemies rejoice over me. Lord, my God, I cried out to You, and You healed me. Lord, You have raised up my soul from the grave; You have kept me alive, that I should not descend to the pit. Sing to the Lord, His pious ones, and give thanks to His holy Name. For His anger endures but a moment, when He is conciliated there is life. In the evening one lies down weeping, but joy will come in the morning. In my security I thought, "I shall never falter." But, Lord, all is by Your favor – You supported my greatness with might; when You concealed Your countenance, I was alarmed. I called to You, O Lord, and I appealed to my Lord. What gain is there in my death, in my going down to the grave? Will the dust praise You? Will it proclaim Your truth? Lord, hear and be gracious to me; Lord, be my Helper! You have turned my mourning into dancing; You have transformed my lament and girded me with joy. Therefore my soul shall sing to You and not be stilled; Lord my God, I will thank You forever.

Printed in Dunstable, United Kingdom